My first computer guide

Chris Oxlade

Heinemann
LIBRARY

www.heinemann.co.uk/library

Visit our website to find out more information about Heinemann Library books.

To order:

☎ Phone 44 (0) 1865 888066

▤ Send a fax to 44 (0) 1865 314091

▭ Visit the Heinemann Bookshop at www.heinemann.co.uk/library to browse our catalogue and order online.

First published in Great Britain by Heinemann Library, Halley Court, Jordan Hill, Oxford OX2 8EJ, part of Harcourt Education.
Heinemann is a registered trademark of Harcourt Education Ltd.

© Harcourt Education Ltd 2007
First published in paperback in 2008
The moral right of the proprietor has been asserted.

Editorial: Isabel Thomas, Charlotte Guillain and Diyan Leake
Design: Philippa Jenkins
Illustrations: Tower Designs (UK) Ltd
Picture Research: Melissa Allison
Production: Duncan Gilbert

Originated by Dot Gradations
Printed and bound in China by South China Printing Co. Ltd

ISBN 978 0 431 90696 6 (hardback)
11 10 09 08 07
10 9 8 7 6 5 4 3 2 1

ISBN 978 0 431 90701 7 (paperback)
12 11 10 09 08
10 9 8 7 6 5 4 3 2 1

British Library Cataloguing in Publication Data
Oxlade, Chris
  My first computer guide. - (My First Computer Guides)
  1. Computers - Juvenile literature
  I. Title
  004

A full catalogue record for this book is available from the British Library.

Acknowledgements
The publishers would like to thank the following for permission to reproduce photographs: Alamy pp. **10** left (archivberlin Fotoagentur GmbH), **28** (Charles Bowman), **5** right and **21** (ImageDJ); Apple Computer, Inc. p. **4**; Corbis pp. **6** (LWA-Dann Tardif), **10** (Michael Prince), **19** (LWA- JDC), **27** (Royalty-Free), **29** (Charles O'Rear); Getty Images pp. **18-19** (Photodisc); Harcourt Education Ltd pp. **5** bottom, **6/7**, **8/9**, **20**, **25** (Tudor Photography), **26** (Heinemann Explore); Lexmark International p. **5** left; Internet Explorer is a registered trademark of Microsoft Corporation in the United States and United Kingdom p. **13** left; Mozilla.org p. **13** right and **14**; PhotoEdit Inc/Bill Aron p. **23**; Sony Europe p. **5** top.

Cover photograph of optical computer mouse, reproduced with permission of Corbis (William Whitehurst).

The publishers would like to thank Robert Eiffert for his assistance in the preparation of this book.

Every effort has been made to contact copyright holders of any material reproduced in this book. Any omissions will be rectified in subsequent printings if notice is given to the publishers.

Contents

Some words are shown in bold, **like this**. You can find
out what they mean by looking in the glossary.

Learning about computers

screen (monitor)

keyboard

mouse

A computer is a special type of machine.
It can do many different jobs.

This computer is called a laptop computer or notebook computer.

scanner

printer

These machines plug into the computer.

camera

5

How we use computers

We use computers at school, at home and at work. They help us with writing, drawing and painting, maths, sending messages, and finding information.

Computers help us to work on projects.

We can also use computers to store things. We can store photographs, music and videos on a computer. Many people use computers to play games.

On and off

You have to press the power switch to turn a computer on before you can use it. It takes a few seconds to start up.

Registered Users:

User Name

Password | Enter

You might have to type in a password before you can start using the computer.

When you have finished using a computer, you must shut it down. You shut down the computer by clicking on a button. You do not press the power switch to turn off the computer.

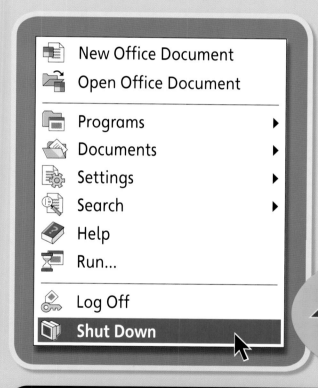

New Office Document
Open Office Document

Programs ▶
Documents ▶
Settings ▶
Search ▶
Help
Run...

Log Off
Shut Down

When you click on the "Shut Down" button on the screen, the computer will turn itself off.

STAY SAFE   X

 Never turn off a computer without shutting down first. Never pull out any plugs while the computer is on.

Moving a mouse

You use the **mouse** to make the computer do things. The mouse makes a pointer move about on the screen. You can click on things and move things with the mouse.

The mouse looks like a real mouse, with a long tail.

Sometimes you need one click. Sometimes you need to click twice quickly. This is called a double-click.

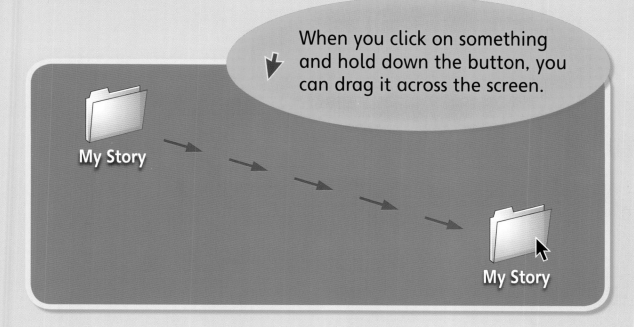

When you click on something and hold down the button, you can drag it across the screen.

My Story

My Story

Activity

Go to a computer and practise moving the mouse in different directions. Watch the pointer on the screen to see how it is moving.

Computer programs

A computer **program** lets us do things with a computer. A word processor program lets us write words and sentences using the keyboard. A painting program lets us make pictures on the screen.

A painting program has buttons we can use for making a picture.

Some programs let us look at information or sort it out. Other programs let us write or speak to other people. Games programs let us play on the computer.

These programs let us look at websites on the Internet.

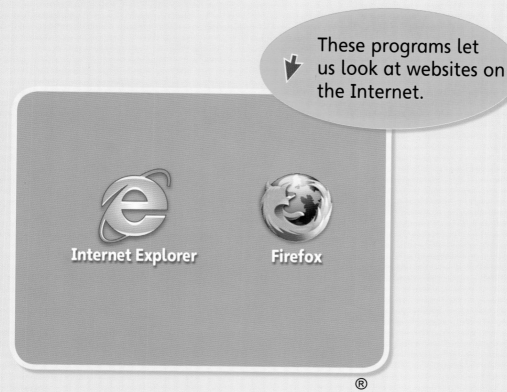

Internet Explorer   Firefox

®

On your desktop

After the computer has started up, you see the **desktop**. On the desktop are small pictures called **icons**.

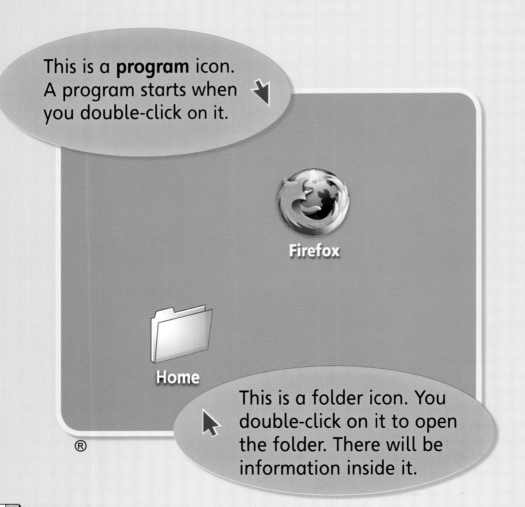

This is a **program** icon. A program starts when you double-click on it.

Firefox

Home

This is a folder icon. You double-click on it to open the folder. There will be information inside it.

The button to shut down your computer is on the desktop. There is also a trash or recycling bin. You can put work you no longer need in here.

Trash

Recycle Bin

 STAY SAFE **X**

 On some computers, you can throw away things on the desktop by dragging them into the trash bin. Make sure you do not do this by accident.

Using windows

When you open a folder or start a **program**, a box appears on the screen. This box is called a **window**. You can have many windows open on the desktop at the same time.

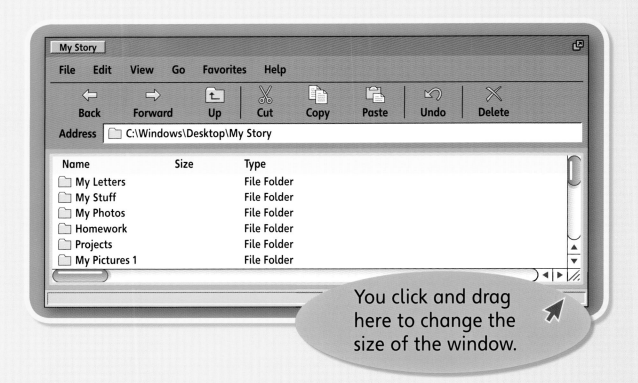

You click and drag here to change the size of the window.

When you open a window, there are **menus** on the screen. These menus let you choose what you want to do. Click on your choice with the **mouse**.

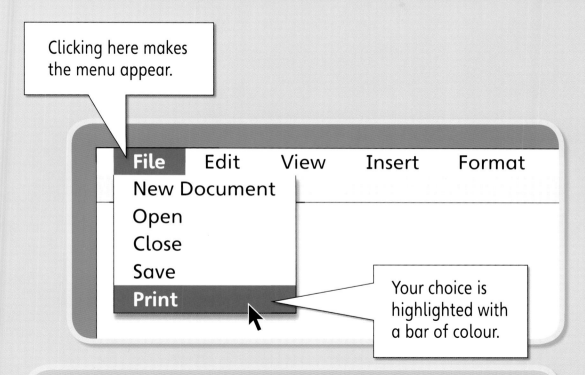

Clicking here makes the menu appear.

File	Edit	View	Insert	Format

New Document
Open
Close
Save
Print

Your choice is highlighted with a bar of colour.

Activity

To close a window down, click on the ⊠ **icon** in the top corner. Now try to hide a window without closing it. You click on the ▭ icon in the top corner.

Putting stuff in

We put information into a computer as we work on it. The information is called **data**. We put in letters and numbers with the keyboard. Pressing keys also makes the computer do things, such as moving the page up and down.

number keys

letter keys

Press the "Shift" key to get capital letters.

Press the space bar to add spaces between words.

Press the "Delete" key to rub out a letter or number.

STAY SAFE ☒

⚠ Always sit upright at a desk while you are using a computer. The screen and keyboard should be straight ahead of you.

More input

There are many ways of putting **data** into a computer. The data can be stored on the computer.

A **digital camera** puts photographs into the computer. Information goes along a cable into the computer.

cable

A scanner is a machine that makes a copy of something. You can put photographs, pictures and paintings in a scanner. The scanner turns them into information that you can store on the computer.

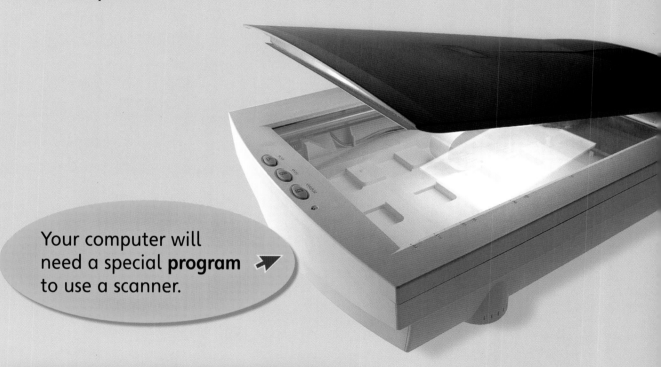

Your computer will need a special **program** to use a scanner.

Printing out

We often want to print out the information we see on the screen. We do this with a printer. The printer makes a copy of the information on paper.

Click the "Print" button when you want to print.

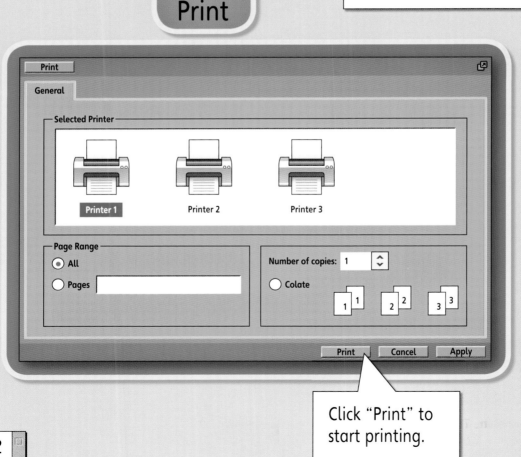

Print			
General			

Selected Printer

Printer 1   Printer 2   Printer 3

Page Range
- ● All
- ○ Pages

Number of copies: 1

- ○ Colate

1 1   2 2   3 3

Print   Cancel   Apply

Click "Print" to start printing.

Always ask your teacher or another adult before you print things out. There might be rules to follow so that paper and ink are not wasted.

Saving and opening

Always save your work before shutting down the computer. Then you can get it back later. The work is saved as a file in the computer.

Choose where you want to put the file here.

Files are stored in folders on the computer. You might have your own folder.

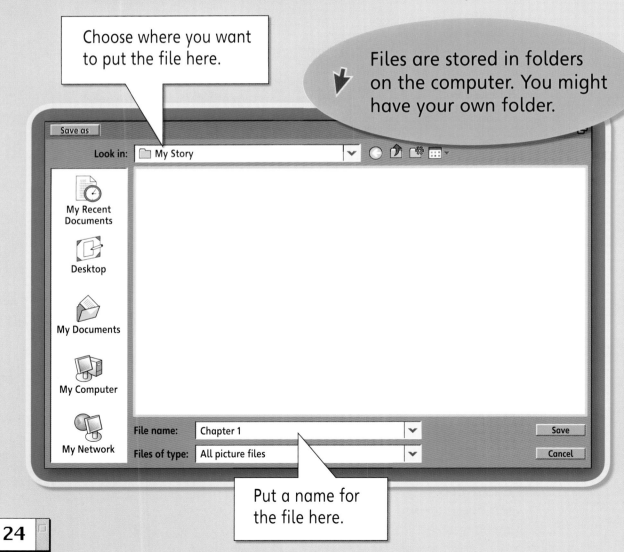

Put a name for the file here.

To find work you have saved, click on the "Open" button. This opens a **window**. The window helps you find your file.

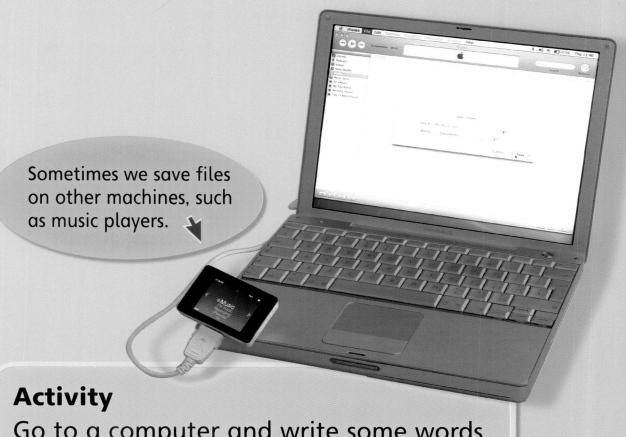

Sometimes we save files on other machines, such as music players.

Activity

Go to a computer and write some words in a word processor **program**. Save the file and close the word processor window. Can you find the file and open it again?

Following instructions

A computer needs a list of instructions to tell it what to do. A computer **program**, such as a word processor or painting program, is a list of instructions. The computer follows the instructions.

The computer follows a program so that you can play a game.

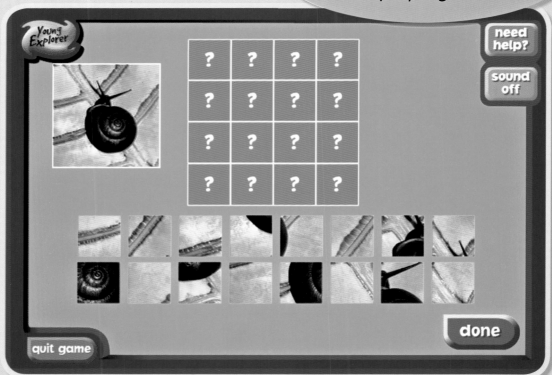

Changing the program makes a computer do a different job. We can make a computer do almost any job we like, from playing games to flying an aircraft.

Looking inside

This is what we would see if we could look inside a computer.

This is a motherboard. Most parts of the computer are attached to this board.

Memory chips remember information when the computer is switched on.

fan

Computers are made up of many parts that work together. Computers help us to work much more quickly and easily. We can have a lot of fun using computers!

The processor is like the computer's brain. It does calculations and moves information around in the memory. It can do millions of sums in a second.

STAY SAFE   **X**

⚠ Never open a computer case. You could break the small parts inside, and the electricity could hurt you.

Fun facts about computers

- The first computers were huge. One computer could fill a whole room!

- The first **mouse** was invented in 1964. It was made of wood and had two metal wheels!

More books to read

Computer Wizards: Windows Magic, Claire Pye and Ruth Cassidy (Watts, 2004)

Computer Basics (Letts, 2000)

Glossary

data information that you put into a computer

desktop area on a computer screen showing folders and programs

digital camera camera that takes photographs that can be put onto computers

icon small picture on a computer screen

menu list of choices that are shown on a computer screen

mouse tool attached to a computer, used to point and click on the screen.

program set of instructions that tells a computer what to do

window a box on the screen that gives you a choice of what to do

Index